The Words That Saved Me

Sarah Mozer

For all the brave souls navigating the ocean of chronic illness.

For my parents for keeping me afloat.

Contents

Introduction

Aged 15, I was intelligent and ambitious, with aspirations to study architecture or engineering, to travel, and to live a free and fun life; when I came back from a school trip to Barcelona with a virus that never went away.

Aged 28, I'm still trying to figure out how to heal from an illness that has tightened its grip on my body and refused to let go for the last 13 years, stealing so much of my life along the way.

In those 13 years I saw my health slowly decline, despite trying countless treatments and alternative therapies, (there is currently no known cure and little funding to find one), until I reached a point of being completely bed bound, reliant on my family for everything, including being washed and fed, too unwell for conversation, TV, podcasts, or any other form of entertainment or distraction. I spent hours alone in my bed stuck in my head with only what I could come up with in my imagination to get me through each day. I fell into a deep depression and no longer wanted to live because I had such a low quality of life.

This is when I first started writing my poems, I needed a place to get out some of the pain I experienced, so as I lay there, I started writing poems in my head and when I had the energy, I would type a few lines at a time into the notes section on my phone. After spending 9 months surviving this darkness I slowly began to see some small improvements in my health, I could feed myself lying down, I could walk to the toilet instead of being wheeled in a chair, I could sit up for a few minutes. I was also working extremely hard on my mental health, trying to find some sort of peace with my situation, starting to realise that fighting it was only causing me more suffering, but not yet knowing how to reach any form of acceptance or peace with a life and body I so desperately hated. I started writing poems that were the words I needed to hear to help me get through my situation, writing with kindness and compassion and trying to learn how to give that to myself. Hating myself for the pain I was in did not make it any better, maybe loving myself would. I wrote about the change in perspective I wanted to find.

The small changes in my mental and physical health allowed me to find tiny sparks of hope, which grew as I continued to make small improvements over the next few months and eventually years and could see the possibility of a lighter future.

It is a daily practice, trying to find peace & acceptance and joy & gratitude in a life I would never have chosen. I'm still learning to be kind to myself, to value myself and to have hope for a better future. I think I found writing at a time when I needed it, it gave me a purpose and the possibility of a future, it made me feel like a part of me could exist beyond my four walls even when I could not. The idea that I could have a book one day may well have saved my life.

I hope the words in this book speak to you in some way, I hope they make you feel the things I felt and understand the experiences I had, opening your eyes to the pain of a life with severe chronic illness.

May they remind you that even during the darkest times in life there is a place of peace within us, and that happiness, contentment and light can and will return.

Most of all though, I hope that whatever you are going through in life and whatever your circumstances that by sharing these pieces of me I can help you in some small way too.

Darkness

Lost soul

Coloured in black

all my light scribbled out,

darkness black as a starless night.

No Northern star,

no shining moon.

A lost soul

with no way back to myself

Frayed

How much can I endure?

When is enough enough?

At what point will it all become too much.

I try

And I try

Holding on to threads of hope

As they fray to single strands,

I can't fight this fight forever

Reflection

How does the girl in the mirror

look exactly the same,

when inside she is someone else entirely.

Her eyes still shine brightly,

despite the horrors she has witnessed.

She stands tall

baring no sign of weariness

from the weight that has been thrust upon her,

no cuts or bruises

from all the times she has been torn apart,

undamaged by the hurricane

tearing its way through her life.

This girl has climbed her way out of the jaws of hell

experiencing pain like no other,

But she stares back at me,

Entirely unchanged

Balancing

Walking on a knife's edge

always afraid to fall,

only takes one wrong step,

And everything comes crashing down.

Thoughts On Pain

Some days all there is is pain,
and that's okay too.

Maybe you have not experienced the pain
or loss of illness,
but pain and loss
themselves are universal.

It's not your fault.
It's not your fault.
It's not your fault.

A Girl Stuck In A Bed

Hollowed out,

an empty shell of who she was.

Creative bright and funny,

replaced by

More tests,

More illnesses,

Medical results,

and readings on charts.

An ever growing list of diagnoses.

Pain where once there was joy,

endless tears where once there was laughter.

The girl who would do anything for anyone

now dependent on everyone for everything.

All the things she was

and all she hoped to be,

But now,

just a girl

stuck

in a bed

Breaking Point

My body was screaming at me to stop

but I did not speak the same language,

so I did not stop,

Until it was too late

Spoonless

She was careless with her spoons,

leaving a trail of them behind her every time she

left the house.

Spoons left in cafes, parks and shops,

spoons in hospitals

and on holidays.

Spoons left in her paintings

and in the books she read,

she gave spoons to strangers

and even more to her friends.

She kept giving away too many spoons,

no one told her

She was supposed to take them back

* The spoon theory is a metaphor used to describe the amount
of energy available for daily activities and tasks.

Each spoon represents a percentage of that day's energy and if
you give away too many you have fewer on subsequent days.

Diluted

I've been punched in the gut again

by the life I yearn for,

but can not have.

Tears flow,

Tears of loss and longing,

desperate to experience every flavour of life

but stuck with the diluted version.

'These are the best years of your life,'

they say,

The years of freedom, adventure and discovery.

Then please tell me,

why are mine wasted like this?

Stuck in these four walls

Shadow

Days and weeks pass,

The world keeps spinning,

A world she is no longer in.

People living their lives,

Moving on.

She fades away,

Forgotten.

Where once there stood a girl,

Now there's just a shadow.

Vultures

The vultures circled overhead.

They clawed away

at any shreds of energy that remained

and left her crumpled body

there to fade away

Heavy

And somehow I'm drowning again.
Just when I thought I'd learnt how to swim,
learnt how to keep my head above the water.

Sinking to the depths of the ocean
pulled into the murky water
and tangles of knotted weeds.
Heavy with the weight of this life.

Far from where I want to be
it's where I find myself once more.
Lost in a hidden world
of crushing darkness and quiet.

Contradiction

I want to accept this

to surrender and find peace,

But I also want to fight it with every ounce of my

being.

To fight off the illness that won't release its grip,

and I don't know how to do both at the same time

Survived

Life tried to make her angry,
she found the strength to remain calm.

Life tried to harden her heart,
she chose to keep it soft.

Life tried to break her apart,
she glued all of her pieces back together.

Life tried to take everything from her,
she never forgot all she still had.

Life knocked her down over and over again,
she picked herself back up every single time.

Life tried to fill her with despair,
she filled herself up with hope.

Life tried to make her believe it wasn't worth living,
she fought her way through every day.

She survived.

Sidelines

I fill my head with noise,

with other people's lives

with other people's stories

to drown out the quiet of my days,

the empty space in my life

I fill it

with their words,

their experiences,

their joys.

To escape from the slowed down time,

the repetition

and mundanity

of a life lived from the sidelines

Rock And Roll

You don't need to keep rolling that rock uphill

over and over again.

Endlessly pushing,

but getting no closer to the top.

Life is not a Greek myth;

you can step aside

and just let it roll away

Bed Rest

No one ever says

'Well done for resting',

But it's the hardest thing

I've ever had to do.

To spend all day

in my bed

stuck in my head,

eyes closed

body still.

The only way to pass the time

with what I come up with

in my mind.

My body needs to be here,

but my heart,

it longs to be elsewhere

An Empty Day Part I

Another empty day looms;

hours to fill

but no energy to fill them.

Stuck in my own head

and starved of conversation

or stimulation.

No books

No music

No films or TV.

Stuck in these same four walls.

There's a whole world out there;

taunting me

with its new people

and experiences.

Familiar faces

and far off places.

All the things I could see and do

but no,

I am imprisoned in this empty room

An Empty Day Part 2

An empty day can still find ways to be filled;

fill it with gratitude for people who love you,

the kindness of strangers.

With four legged friends who stand guard by your

side,

with hugs

and silent company.

The presence of meditation

and the endlessness of your imagination.

Taste every mouthful you eat,

feel every breath that you take.

Watch the sky and the trees

because don't forget

that fourth wall is actually a window.

The day may seem long

and it may be difficult to fill.

But it's yours to have,

so don't let it be empty

Belonging

These walls

these confines

and restraints;

they are not for her.

She does not belong here.

She belongs with nothing but sky above her

and nothing but the ground beneath her feet.

She belongs with the wind in her hair

and the sun on her skin.

She belongs in mountains and meadows and

streams.

She belongs with the sand between her toes

and the taste of the salty sea air,

with vast open fields

and the comforting darkness of woodlands,

with grass and trees and flowers,

embraced by nature.

She belongs there

She longs to be there

Four Walls

At the time she was most ready to grow

her world just kept getting smaller.

From a town

To a street

To a house,

Until all that was left

was just a room.

Four walls bursting at the seams

with all her unlived plans and dreams

Winter

And suddenly it was winter,
all her leaves had fallen.
Her branches standing bare,
she looked tired and worn
empty of life.

But her roots were strong;
grounding her to hope and courage,
nurturing her with all she needed.
She could withstand all knocks
and all beatings,
however unexpected they may be.
So that when her season comes,
she would blossom
into the beautiful and strong being
that had stood there all along

Unsaid

So many things left unspoken.

Left unsaid.

The words.

The phrases.

Building up.

The conversations I've had.

Only in my head.

My brain overflows.

Some days it could burst.

With all that I would like to say.

Friends and family

I'm desperate to speak to.

But all I have is quiet.

Solitude.

No energy to form these words.

So they remain unspoken.

Remain unsaid.

Lighthouse

However dark the day may be

I know I can survive,

I can weather any storm,

ride waves of the roughest seas,

because I look out

and I can always see

the light you shine for me.

My lighthouse,

beaming bright,

guiding me home

keeping me safe

and lighting the path

back to shore

Beside Me

If I could have chosen any path in life

there's not a part of me

that would walk this one.

But given the choice

every single time

I'd choose the same people

walking it beside me.

Because the days on which I can not stand

or take another single step,

they hold me up,

they carry me through,

until I find my feet again

The Words I
Need To Hear

The Words I Need To Hear

I'm sorry things are hard for you

I'm sorry that you are suffering and in pain

I'm sorry that you are unable

to do so many things that you wish you could.

I know that it hurts you so much

and it's okay to feel that way,

your feelings are always valid.

But please remember:

you will get there

you will get to that place

you are working so hard for.

This is only temporary.

Nothing is forever.

I am so so proud of you for keeping going through

it all

Keep Going

Heal yourself with kindness;

you are not broken

you did not choose this.

Heal yourself with love;

pour until you are overflowing.

Heal yourself with patience;

you have no expiration

there is no rush.

Heal yourself with courage;

when every part of you says give up

find the part that says keep going

Patience

While you are lying there

feeling like you are doing nothing,

every cell in your body

every fibre of your being

is instinctively working away,

fighting a battle you cannot see

but that you will undoubtedly win.

So lie still.

Rest,

and be reassured:

that your strength will return

your energy will replenish

you will recover.

Healing takes patience

Enough

There is no such thing as doing 'enough' in a day,
whatever you're able to do is enough.
You don't need to do 'enough' before you can rest,
if you need to rest
then rest.
You always have permission.

The most important thing to focus on
is giving yourself what you need
to heal and recover.
Everything else can wait.

I See You

You who cannot leave the house
You who cannot leave your bed
You who cannot see your friends
or your family
You who cannot work
You who cannot be a part of the world
in the way you'd like.

I need you to know:
You are valued
You will always be a part of this world
You are not forgotten
I see you

Constant Motion

Do not fear the future

for you do not know what it holds,

life is in constant motion

each moment different from the next.

So when what's around the corner

leaves you filled with fear.

Remember,

tomorrow will not be as today

This Moment

Just focus

on this moment

it's the only one there is,

the only one that's real.

Whatever

is happening

in this moment

is exactly what

is supposed

to be happening.

Faith

On the days where you feel like
you cannot stay in this bed,
not a minute longer.
Stay in this room
another second.

Remember why you're here.
Remember all the hours you've spent
resting
healing.
Do not let them go to waste,
you can get through these difficult days
you've done so well so far.

Have faith
Have patience
You will get there

I know it's so hard to find faith from nowhere

drawing it out of thin air,

but keep doing that.

Keep believing that this resting will be worth it

it will pay off.

You'll get the life you are desperately yearning for.

Have faith

Have patience

You will get there

Proud

I am proud of you for every time
you have chosen to sit with your emotions
instead of running from them.
I am proud of you for every time
you have chosen compassion over criticism,
for every time you have chosen positivity over
negativity.
I am proud of you for learning to trust in yourself
again,
for the times you have found the courage
to be open and vulnerable.
I am proud of all the changes you make every day
in your brain,
the ones only I can see.
For every time you choose to go right instead of
left.
I'm proud of you for your endless persistence and
perseverance,
I am so very proud of you

Breath By Breath

There will be a day when things are better

but if you give up now

you'll never reach it.

Take things one day at a time

one hour

or even one breath.

You have survived this far.

Do not give up.

Giving up is not an option.

Safe

You are safe.

It may feel like the whole world is out to get you,

but you are safe.

It may feel like everything is a threat,

but still,

you are safe.

When even your own brain

feels like a danger,

take a moment,

leave those thoughts

for they are just words

let go of their meaning.

When even your own body

feels like a danger,

step back from your symptoms

they are just sensations

energy flowing through you

let go of their meaning.

Sometimes this will feel impossible,

sometimes merely existing will feel impossible

and in those moments

know that I am here,

you will find your way out.

You are safe.

The Ghosts Of My Worst Days

The ghosts of my worst days
come back to haunt me.
The pain drifts in,
the sadness fills my bones
until I'm heavy
with the weight of them.
The memories of that time
reappearing in my brain
shadows of a time that doesn't seem real.

These memories are mine
but the person wasn't me.

This person,
she finds space in my mind
to show me her pain.
She needs me to see her,
to sit with her,
tell her it's okay.

And I find space in my heart

to show her my love;

a love I didn't know how to give

when she needed it most.

'I'm sorry you went through that' I say.

'I'm sorry you were in so much pain you didn't

know what else to do'

'Thank you for keeping on going'

'Thank you for surviving when you didn't think you

could'

'I forgive you' I say.

'I love you.'

Compassion

It's so easy to blame yourself

and so difficult to forgive,

but my darling girl

how many times must I tell you;

none of this is your fault.

Do not hate your body

for something it had no choice in,

do not cause it more harm or unnecessary pain.

You will not fix something broken by damaging it

more.

You must learn to show it gentle tenderness

the way you would any other suffering being,

and to treat it with compassion and understanding

the way you would any other human,

you deserve that too

My Dear Little Fighter

My dear little fighter,

Your armour may not be shining metal,
but I see you put it on each day.
Your weapons may not be guns or swords,
but I see your continued fight.

I see your courage for getting up each day
when it feels like there's no point.
I see your resilience for finding new hope
when it has been dashed so many times before.
I see your bravery for trying new things
however much they scare you.
I see your strength for fighting the daily battle with
your own brain.

And though this war may seem like it has no end
You are mighty
You are fierce

So I know

One day

You will be triumphant

Whole

You are whole.

It is impossible for you to be

anything other than whole,

anything other than complete.

In the same way that a tree

does not wonder

if it is doing a good job of being a tree,

it simply *is* a tree;

you don't need to wonder

if you are doing a good job of being you.

You simply *are* you.

You are always exactly as you are supposed to be.

Stardust And Magic

If all you did today was exist,

then to exist was your purpose.

Maybe it seems like a waste,

but you are here for a reason.

The universe created you

from stardust

and magic.

And maybe right now

the reason doesn't seem clear,

but one day

you will see:

that your simple existence is your

purpose.

You being alive

is the meaning of your life

Spark Of Hope

Roaring Fire Within You

Hold on to that tiny spark of hope

however small it may be.

Nurture it.

Nourish it.

Watch it grow

and glow

into the roaring fire within you

Shutters

You may not have the life you desire

but you can choose to live it

or watch it pass you by.

Just because you can only see the world

through the window

does not mean that you are not a part of it.

Do not lock yourself inside

or close down your shutters,

be open to what you can still see,

feel the warmth of the sunlight.

Let the world in.

Spring

The first tentative shoots emerge,

buds bloom,

leaves begin to uncurl.

Colour bursts from the

bleakness.

The world has re-awoken

and so have I

You Are Never Alone

How can we ever be alone if we are truly
with ourselves?

Be with every breath and heartbeat
Be with every thought and feeling

Let these be your company
Let these be your solace

You are *never* alone

Acceptance

No thought or feeling is good or bad until
you decide it is.

When sadness comes knocking
do not barricade it at the door,
invite it in.

When thoughts feel unbearable
do not fight them away,
sit beside them.

When pain sears through every part of your being
look it in the eye,
and allow it to be exactly as it is.

Two Paths

There are two paths that lead you to what's truly important in life:

The first is getting everything you ever wanted and finding out it still hasn't made you happy.

The second is to lose something or someone hugely important to you and have your whole world fall apart.

It's funny how two such opposite situations can both lead us to the same realisations.

How they can both block out all the noise and open our eyes to what matters

Comfort Blanket

We tell ourselves we have control

but it's a total illusion.

A comfort blanket

carried round

that slowly suffocates instead.

So put it down,

and let it go,

look behind that curtain.

Allow yourself to lose control

be left with doubt instead.

The future will unfold itself

in whatever way it chooses.

There will always be uncertainty,

we will never have control.

To accept that

and be at peace with it

is where true comfort can be found

Surrender

Fighting the present moment

is a fight you can never win,

you can resist with all your strength

but it's an impossible battle,

like trying to make a river flow upstream.

Anger

frustration

and sadness

will not help you here.

Put down those weapons

they will only cause you more pain.

Instead;

choose acceptance,

choose peace.

Find the strength

to surrender to this moment

exactly as it is

Deck Of Cards

Asking 'Why me?'

Is as futile as asking 'Why not me?'

Not everything happens for a reason.

There isn't always logic or fairness,

bad things can happen to good people.

A bad day or month or year

do not mean you aren't trying hard enough

or that you have done anything wrong.

Life is simply a series of random events

one after the other.

No pattern

and no one to blame.

Just a deck of cards strewn across the table

Float

Lost in an ocean of uncertainty

Battered by relentless currents

Pushed to the ocean floor

Fighting to reach the surface

I stop fighting.

I spread my arms

And I float

And I breathe

Light surrounds me

The waves carry me

And I am free

Turn Up

This other life
you were 'supposed to have'
never happened
isn't real,
there is no parallel existence
no world where you never got ill.

Maybe there are no 'supposed to's
maybe there's only have or have not,
and this is the life you have my dear
you only get to live it once.

Stop wishing for that imagined one,
it's time to let it go
its time to live in the present
and turn up for the one that's real.

Instagram Squares

Every square is a window
but you'll never see inside the full house,
you'll never see what's hiding
just out of your sight.

The cupboards are spilling over
with old mistakes and regrets
and the bookshelves are stacked high
with insecurities and worries.
There's a pile of dirty laundry
and a bed that's never made,
bad days are tucked away in corners
those ones you'd rather just forget.

Any imperfections,
the windows filter them all out.
This house is far from perfect
but through its square shaped windows
you would never know.

Because yes these squares

make a pretty picture

they'll just never show you

the whole story.

Back To The Present

1. Take 5 deep breaths
2. Feel the breaths as they flow through your body
3. Feel the surface you're on
4. Feel the physical sensations of the emotion
5. Where in the body can you feel it?

   What colour is it?

   What shape is it?

   What size is it?
6. Sink into that sensation fully
7. Give it all of your love and compassion

My Broken Pieces

Some days I notice the first chip.

Some days the crack goes deeper.

Some days I fall apart entirely.

But I am learning to put back together

my own broken pieces

Head In The Sand

It's easier to keep my head in the sand.
It's easier to keep my heart buried away
in a place it can't get hurt,
to hide from the pain
I carry within me.

Easier than feeling it
than facing it.
But to face it is to heal it.

So I will dig away at the sand
find my buried heart
find my buried pain.

I will feel all the things
I've been too afraid to feel.

I will set them free
I will set myself free

I will heal

Stop Judging

Nobody will ever judge you

as harshly

as you've judged yourself.

Nobody has the right

to judge you,

including yourself

Be Proud

In a world

that places value

on a list

of physical achievements,

it's easy to feel

like you are falling short

when you spend so many hours resting;

non-doing

rather than doing,

listening to your body

not following your heart,

learning to say no instead of yes.

Never underestimate

the greatness of these achievements.

They take skill and self-discipline

in their own unique way.

Just because there is no certificate

to frame on your wall,

no photo for social media.

Just because

your achievements can't be measured

or graded

it does not make their value any less.

Be proud.

Cocoon

You can not change your situation

but you can change the way that you see it:

Maybe these walls are not a prison

but an embrace,

a cocoon

keeping you safe,

giving you time to rest

and to heal.

So soften in their grip

and trust in their protection.

They will take care of you

until your strength returns.

And trust that they will know

when the time is right

for you to emerge once more.

All The Things I Am But Cannot Be

Artist

Bookworm

Traveller

Gardener

Baker

Dog walker

Friend

Sister

Daughter

My true self

These are the things I am

Even if I cannot be them right now

Even when I feel limited and shrunken

I am more than my illness

And always will be

The Stories We Tell Ourselves

The brain makes up its own stories
it can tell you what it likes,
so be careful of the things you think
will they do you help or harm.

Fairy-tales and make believe
are not just the stuff of books.
When you make up a story
in your mind
and read it everyday,
one day you'll forget it's fiction
and it will become real too.

So tell yourself the good ones,
that add magic to your life.
Where the princess doesn't need saving
because she knows how to save herself.
Where she trusts in her own strength
and knows she can get through this.

All the monsters that she's facing
she has the courage to defeat.

Maybe there's no such thing
as happily ever after,
and maybe that's okay
when you can believe
in the better days ahead.
Choosing to tell yourself the story
of the life you'll one day live.

Who I Am

I don't know who I am anymore,

but maybe that's okay.

I'm not the girl I was before,

but maybe that's okay.

Maybe this is my chance to grow

to find a new

and deeper

sense of self.

To find who I was supposed to be all along

but who I never thought to search for.

I get to choose who I am.

To rebuild myself.

To put my pieces

back together

and to know that I am complete.

Afraid But Brave

I'm afraid.

Afraid every day that I'll wake up
back in the darkness.
That all it takes is one wrong move
and my fragile progress
will come tumbling down.

Every natural human function has
become alien to me
and it's terrifying learning to do them all again,
to trust my body again
when my brain keeps telling me it's not safe.

But I'm also brave,
because I wake up everyday
and I keep going

Autumn

Autumn is a time for letting go.
The trees let go of their leaves
they float and dance in the breeze.

And I let go of trying to control
things beyond my control,
of fear,
of anger and frustration;
they float and dance away as I breathe

My Story

I don't want to be ashamed anymore

of my physical limitations,

they are neither

my fault

nor

my choice,

and I am doing everything in my power

to change them.

I want to be proud of the person

I've become

not in spite of my illness,

but because of it.

I want to own my story.

Note To Self

When you are thinking of
all the times you fell apart,
make sure you remember
all the times you didn't.

Every Single Time

If I said I'd never lost hope

I would be lying,

I have lost it

over

and

over again.

But I have also found it.

Every.

Single.

Time.

Searching

On the other side of resistance,

there is peace

to be found.

To find it

you have to

stop s e a r c h i n g

Perspective

When you're feeling overwhelmed

and everything seems too much,

just take a step back

and remember:

you are a speck of dust

on a rock

hurtling through the universe,

a blip in the spectrum of time.

So small and inconsequential,

almost impossible that you even exist.

So does this really matter?

No.

Nothing does.

But in a good way.

In a way that lightens that load

you can't put down.

Quietens some of the noise

in a brain that won't be quiet.

Eases some of the pain

that seeps through your bones.

And loosens the grip

of your deepest fears.

Resilience

It's time to change
that voice in my head,
to stop telling myself
I can't get better
because it's been too many years
and I've tried so many things,
none of them have worked.

I will tell myself
I can get better
because even after all these years
and all these setbacks,
I still haven't stopped trying.
And I will always keep trying.
That strength,
that resilience,
that is why I can recover.

Other Side

Don't give up on yourself.

Don't give up on the future that is still waiting for you.

You have gone through so much already,

endured so much hardship,

do not let that be wasted.

Keep going.

One foot in front of the other.

Because this is not forever.

This is only the before,

but there will be an after.

There is so much wonder

waiting for you

on the other side.

And I know you can do it.

Light In Her Eyes

Inextinguishable

There is a light that will never go out
I see it shining from your eyes;
some days it's a single ray,
some days it's the entire sun.

So many things have been taken
but know that this will never be one,
because no matter what you go through
or how dark you feel inside,
nothing will ever extinguish
a light as magnificent as yours.

Light In The Darkness

You did not choose this,

but you can choose:

To smile

To love

To hope

To laugh

To have faith

To keep going

To find strength

To be positive

To live each day

To not give up

To find light in the darkness

Shine On

The star shining next to you

does not make your light

glow any less bright.

Without you,

the universe would never be complete.

Pieces Of Me

There's a piece of me in every word,

every poem,

every page.

I cannot leave this house

but these pieces of me can.

So I hope that there will be

pieces of me

on bookshelves

and coffee tables,

in hearts

and minds.

I hope that pieces of me go

to all the places I can not.

Worthy

In case you need it
here is your reminder
that it's time you stop
mixing up your health
and your worth.

Physical ability
does not determine your worth,
not in any way.

You, my dear, have an innate worth.
Your energy levels may fluctuate
but your worth,
it never does,
never will.

Next Step

If you can't yet believe you can

reach your destination.

Hold on to the belief you can

take the next step.

Glimmer

I feel the kind of gratitude

you can only feel

when you get back

the things you lost

but thought you would never find.

I feel the kind of lightness

you can only feel

when you fall so far into darkness

it seems there is no way out.

And then one day

there's a glimmer.

The Pain Of Letting Go

The pain is different this time.

The tears sound the same,

but the pain is different.

It doesn't erupt

from angry words and thoughts,

from desperation and despair.

It flows from a quiet,

where the thoughts stop,

where there is stillness

and space.

I feel its power deep within.

It is water finally bursting from a dam.

It is a pain of letting go.

Believe

I don't know why I am where I am,

maybe there is no reason or plan.

But I choose to believe

I'm where I'm supposed to be,

because that is the thought

that sets me free.

A Full Life

Living life to the full

does not have to mean

adventure or travel,

new experiences and excitement.

Living life to the full

does not mean

constantly wishing

for things you can't have

or to be some place that you aren't.

It does not mean

lusting over a life

that's not yours.

It means turning up

for each and every day.

Being present

and making the most of each moment.

Wherever they are

and whatever those moments may hold.

A life spent in any way

can be a full one

if you decide to live it fully.

Flowers On A Tuesday Part I

Write to me;
write me letters and poems and songs.

Bring me flowers
just because it's Tuesday.

Cook me dinner,
burn it,
we'll eat it anyway.

Spend all day
snuggled under the duvet with me,
sharing your secrets and dreams
and every night sleeping beside me;
I'll even put up with your snoring.

Find me curled up on the floor crying,
curl up right there next to me.

Laugh with me,

laugh until our stomachs ache

and tears stream down our faces.

Fill my days with joy

simply because

you're in them.

Give me your heart,

and I'll give you mine.

Empty Parts

Emptiness cannot be filled
by longing for more.
To ask 'What is missing from my life?'
Is the wrong question,
you will always find something lacking.

Instead,
ask yourself
'What do I have in life?'
And fill the empty parts of you
with that.

Live

There is no greater reminder

to focus on the process

rather than the outcome

than life itself.

Whose only outcome is an ending,

but whose process is so often missed out on

Happy

How do you know
the things you think you want
will actually make you happy?

Maybe there is happiness to be found
with your life exactly as it is now.

Flowers On A Tuesday Part 2

She said, 'I want someone to love me the way he
loves her.'
'So why not love yourself that way?'
was her reply.

Stop using the mirror
to pick apart your reflection,
instead find the beauty
that no spot
or unwashed hair
could ever mask.

Be the arms
that comfort you
on a dark and lonely night,
and the gentle hands
that wipe away tears
with compassion and kindness.

Forgive your shortcomings and mistakes

in the same way you would

for any other.

Laugh at your own jokes,

even the crap ones.

And buy yourself flowers

just because it's Tuesday.

Tell yourself

how wonderful,

brilliant

and magical you are,

until you believe it to be true.

See the unique value

that only you can bring to this world.

Put yourself on that pedestal.

You And I

We'll build our house together,
our home together,
our lives together.
We'll paint the walls with love
and spill it across every surface.

We'll fill our house
with laughter and memories,
and children and dogs.

We'll plant a garden,
grow our own vegetables and flowers.
We'll plant our hopes
and seeds of our future.

Let's build our life together.
Let's grow old together.
You and I.

Dear Best Friend

Dear best friend,

I hope you see yourself
the way that I see you;
I hope you see
your beauty
and your value,
how it shines from within.

I hope you believe in yourself
the way I believe in you;
that you can see your talents
and find the confidence
to share them.

I hope you talk to yourself
the way I would talk to you;
that the voice in your head is kind,
non-judgemental

and forgiving.

And most of all,

I hope you love yourself

the way I love you;

unconditionally

and always.

Interstellar Exclamation

You give me your light

and I give you mine,

our kind of friendship

has its own special shine.

If the world feels too lonely,

or when darkness looms,

look out of your window

and up at the sky,

because no matter the distance

between you and I,

we are always looking up

at the same moon.

It glows brightly for you

when I can not be there.

An interstellar exclamation

of the bond we'll always share.

Popcorn Paws

Nothing brings me comfort
in the way that you can,
with your weight
and your warmth
and your soft fur under my hand.

I love the way you walk
with your tail swishing high
and the looks that you give
from those heart melting eyes.

You bring me a sense of calm
with your gentle little snores,
and the unique smell
of your popcorn paws.

I love your floppy ears,
your fluffy feet,
and your jiggly ginger beard.

Even if you only love me back,

when I give you food,

I'm okay with that

because you do wonders

for my mood.

You're a special kind of dog

couldn't fetch a ball to save your life,

but you've done an excellent job

of saving mine.

Boxes

I will not bend

to fit into your box.

I will not let you

make me feel smaller than I am.

I am vast,

and boundless.

I am the night sky

filled with stars.

I am oceans

and continents.

I have the entire universe

forever expanding within me;

I am infinite.

I will never be contained

by the box you think is mine.

Power

She often wondered

what she had to offer the world,

what she could bring,

how the world was better with her in.

It was a shame

it took her

so long to realise,

that all she had to do

was be herself;

her wonderful

and irreplaceable self.

Because after all,

no one else

can ever

or will ever

be able to do that.

That's her power.

Opinions

Why is anybody else's opinion of you more

true,

valid,

important,

than your opinion of yourself?

If you know you are

good,

kind,

doing your best,

then trust in your opinion,

and don't let others make you question yourself.

The only opinion of you that matters is *yours*

so make sure it's a kind one

Own It

It's time

to stop living your life

as though

it's an apology

for your existence

and to start living defiantly.

Learning to accept kindness

and goodness

with the belief that you deserve it.

Feeling the entirety

of your worth

feeling the certainty that you belong.

Live like you mean it.

Live with intention.

This life is yours,

it's time to own it.

Every Part Of Me

Fall in love with every part of me:

love every scar

and every imperfection.

See the parts that no one else sees

and love me more because of them.

Travel every unexplored pathway

leaving your fingerprints across my body.

Find your way into my heart

and fill it up with love.

Love me when I am just a drop

and when I am the entire ocean.

Love me wholly and inexhaustibly,

I will not settle for less.

Everything Changes

Stop looking to other people
for the approval that you seek.
Stop waiting for their acceptance,
for their praise,
for their love.

It doesn't matter what they think
or what their opinion of you is.
They can never give you
the knowledge and belief
that you are enough
exactly as you are.

They can never give you
what you think you need,
only you can do that.
And once you realise that
and start doing something about it,
once you start looking inside

finding and creating your own self love,

your own acceptance,

everyone else's opinions of you

stop mattering.

Their words lose their power.

Others' approval,

others' praise

is unimportant

when you have that from within.

Once you know

that you are enough

exactly as you are.

Everything changes.

How To Change The World

Maybe you haven't changed the entire world,

but you've changed the entire world for somebody.

And did you ever think,

maybe that's the same thing?

In Her Orbit

She is the sun:

Dazzling

Blazing

Radiant.

Her light

keeps the whole world alive.

I will forever be

in her orbit

Mother Nature

Her curves rose and fell

like soft snow covered peaks.

Streams forged their way

across her body,

carving out her ripples and ridges.

Wildflowers bloomed across her skin,

growing freely.

She was untamed,

natural,

and beautiful.

Sunshine

Fill yourself up with sunshine,

save it for a rainy day,

so that when your sky clouds over,

there'll always be light

to guide your way.

Summer

Summer is hearing yourself laugh
for the first time in months,
that foreign sound,
that used to be so familiar.

Summer is feeling fresh air on your skin
and the ground on your bare feet.

Summer is watching
glimmers of sun appear
after the darkest of storms.

Summer is hope.

Summer is freedom.

The Words That Saved Me

A sense of identity

when all that I was

got stripped away.

Connection

to those I love

and to you

reading this

feeling the things I feel.

An outlet for pain

that had no other way out.

The words on these pages,

these poems I've written,

they saved me.

Just For Me

The sun shines its nourishing warmth,

the birds sing and soar,

the clouds trail their paths and patterns

across the bluest of skies.

The wind blows gently across my skin.

All of this,

just for me.

I lie here

surrounded by this beauty,

immersed in the peace of this moment.

I lie here knowing

with absolute certainty

that I am the luckiest girl in the world.

My London

I cannot even begin to explain

the bizarreness

of leaving the house

for the first time

in almost 3 years.

How something so nondescript

can become so alien.

Lying on the back seat of the car

I travelled through a city

I've lived in all my life

but have been absent from

for so many years.

My fragile body

bumped and jolted about,

a car journey now feeling

like a turbulent plane ride.

Deep breaths.

Deep breaths.

So focused on just getting through.

And then I opened my eyes.

Trees.

So.

Many.

Trees.

The pure joy at seeing so much green

after the whiteness of my 4 walls.

The London skyline in the distance

as we drive through Hampstead heath.

Regency architecture,

gothic architecture,

beautiful red brick mansions

on tree lined streets.

The BT tower looming over me;

Madame Tussaud's;

giraffes and zebras of London zoo.

Cars,

busses,

people,

streets.

My London.

My city.

My home.

I cannot wait to return to you.

Here You Are

When you are grieving all you have lost,

do not forget to celebrate all you have gained.

Remember to measure

all the ways you have grown

in strength

and courage

and patience.

Count every small step of progress

however insignificant it may feel.

Do not overlook the memories made,

the moments of happiness and joy;

and remember those days

that felt impossible to survive.

Wear them proudly

as a badge of honour,

because here you are

surviving.

You made it through.

Helpful Things

Throughout my years of ill health I've always been keen to hear about and read things that have helped other people, either to recover or reach a better quality of life, in the hope that they may help me too.

With an illness that currently has no known cure, it feels important for me to pay this forward and share the things that have helped me, even in just a small way, in the hope they may also benefit someone else.

I still have a long way to go to reach full health, but some treatments and resources that have helped improve my quality of life and peace of mind are:

- Daily meditation and gratitude practice
- Nutritional therapist specialising in ME/CFS, Lyme disease, mould etc
- Myofunctional therapy
- Upper cervical chiropractor
- Calm app
- Insight Timer app
- RESTORE membership with Sarah Jackson Coaching
- The Gupta Program
- Tara Brach books, podcasts and meditations

- Joe Dispenza books and meditations
- Mindfully Evie blog and books
- Jeff Foster books, YouTube talks and meditations
- EFT
- Breathing techniques including The Buteyko Method, The Breathing App
- Kristin Neff meditations and talks
- Polyvagal theory – particularly Suki Baxter on YouTube
- Energy healing – particularly Prune Harris on YouTube

Printed in Great Britain
by Amazon

27881514R00091